By Gillian Richardson

Chicago, Illinois

Customer service: 888-363-4266
Visit our website at www.raintreelibrary.com
Published by Raintree, a division of Reed Elsevier, Inc.

Library of Congress Cataloging-in-Publication Data
Richardson, Gillian.
  Ecosystems : species, spaces, and relationships / Gillian Richardson.
    v. cm. -- (Science at work)
Includes bibliographical references (p.   ).
Contents: Finding links -- Species -- Spaces -- Relationships -- Science survey -- Fast facts -- Young scientists@work -- Research on your own.
  ISBN 0-7398-6994-9 (lib. bdg.-hardcover)
  1. Biotic communities--Juvenile literature. [1. Biotic communities.]
I. Title. II. Series: Science at work (Chicago, Ill.)
  QH541.14.R53 2003
  577.8'2--dc21

                        2003007264

Printed and bound in the United States of America
1 2 3 4 5 6 7 8 9 0   07 06 05 04 03

About the consultant: Ezra Glenn is a city planner who works for the City of Somerville, Mass., as director of economic development. He has extensive experience in environmental policy and natural resource protection.

Project Coordinator: Janice L. Redlin
Series Editors: Jennifer Nault, Jennifer Mattson
Consultant: Ezra Glenn
Design and Illustration: Warren Clark
Copy Editor: Heather C. Hudak
Layout: Bryan Pezzi
Photo Researchers: Tracey Carruthers, Wendy Cosh

Note to the Reader
Some words are shown in bold, **like this**. You can find out what they mean by looking in the glossary.

Photograph Credits
Every reasonable effort has been made to trace ownership and to obtain permission to reprint copyright material. The publishers would be pleased to have any errors or omissions brought to their attention so that they may be corrected in subsequent printings.

Cover: Desert (**Corel Corporation**), Ladybug (**Corel Corporation**), Forest (**Photos.com**); **Corel Corporation**: pages 2/3BKG, 3B, 4T, 4B, 5TL, 6T, 6B, 7L, 7M, 7MR, 7R, 8T, 10B, 11B, 12T, 12B, 13B, 15R, 19, 21B, 22, 25L, 25R, 27B, 28, 29B, 29L, 29R, 31T, 32L, 32R, 33B, 34T, 37B, 42L, 44-48BKG; **Digital Vision**: pages 33T, 35T; **EyeWire, Inc.**: page 45; **Istock.com**: pages 14T, 31MT; **MaXx Images**: page 21T; **PhotoDisc, Inc.**: pages 5BR, 16R, 23; **Photos.com**: pages 3T, 3L, 5TR, 5BL, 7ML, 10T, 14B, 16L, 18B, 18T, 30, 31MB, 31B, 34B, 35B, 36T, 37T, 40, 41, 41 inset, 42R, 43L, 43R; **Photovault.com**: pages 26T; **Tom Stack & Associates**: pages 4 inset, 17 (Chip & Jill Isenhart), 9 (Inga Spence), 15L (Diana Stratton), 24 (Thomas Kitchin), 26B (Kitchen & Hurst), 27T (John Gerlach), 36B (Erwin & Peggy Bauer), 38B (Jeff Foott), 38T (Ryan C. Taylor), 39 (Tom & Theresa Stack); **Visuals Unlimited**: page 8B (David Wrobel), 11T (George Herben); **Rick Zuegel**: page 13T.

Contents

Have you ever wondered...

how many animals and plants live on Earth,

how humans affect them,

and how it all fits together?

Have you ever watched dominoes topple? Thousands of small tiles are arranged in an elaborate pattern. Each piece depends on another piece—when the first piece is pushed over, it knocks over the next, and so on. They all tumble over, one after the other.

Think about an ecosystem, which is a community of living things sharing a habitat, in a similar way. Everything is connected. Each **species** depends on the others to survive. Whatever happens to one member happens to the whole community. They are **interdependent**.

Earth is a collection of ecosystems. Scientists are still learning what keeps Earth's large community of living things and its habitats working in balance with each other.

FINDING LINKS

Careers

Would you like to understand how plants and animals live? Perhaps you would like to help them survive in nature? Can you imagine creating new environments that improve how people and wildlife live together? You might want to consider becoming a biologist, a conservation officer, or an environmental planner.

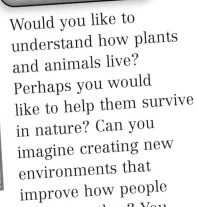

The Environment

An ecosystem consists of **organisms** interacting with each other and their environment. All of the members of an ecosystem affect and depend on each other for survival. Their interactions tend to lead to stability. However, sudden changes—such as the arrival of a new species or the extinction of a species—can put the whole ecosystem at risk.

Society

People and nature are closely linked. Animals and plants often share the same space. Events that affect an animal or plant species can also affect the people sharing the space with these species.

Technology

Scientists collect data to understand how organisms live in the wild. This data can be used to help organisms survive in a changing world. Technology allows scientists to duplicate natural environments and study nature up close.

Species

"It's alive."

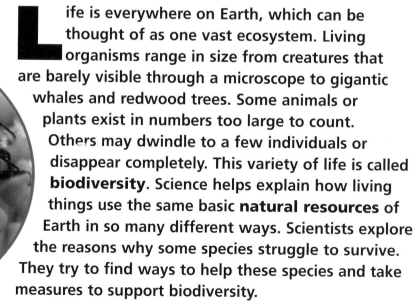

life is everywhere on Earth, which can be thought of as one vast ecosystem. Living organisms range in size from creatures that are barely visible through a microscope to gigantic whales and redwood trees. Some animals or plants exist in numbers too large to count. Others may dwindle to a few individuals or disappear completely. This variety of life is called **biodiversity**. Science helps explain how living things use the same basic **natural resources** of Earth in so many different ways. Scientists explore the reasons why some species struggle to survive. They try to find ways to help these species and take measures to support biodiversity.

What organisms form an ecosystem?

An organism is any living thing. Every organism follows a life cycle. It is born, it grows, and it reproduces. Every organism ages and eventually dies. Then, the new generation experiences the life cycle, so each species continues to exist.

A daisy and a massive blue whale are both organisms. Though the daisy and the whale are both alive, they are very different from each other. Scientists have developed a system, called **classification**, that sorts organisms based on their differences and similarities. Scientists use classification to help them organize information they collect about living things.

Of the five main kingdoms into which scientists divide organisms, the plant kingdom and the animal kingdom are probably the most familiar. Within each kingdom, scientists divide the organisms again into groups and subgroups so that the members of each smaller group have more and more things in common. Within the animal kingdom, there are two main groups: the vertebrates, or animals with backbones, and invertebrates, or animals without backbones.

BYTE-SIZED FACT

It is sometimes helpful to refer to an animal by what it eats. A lion is a mammal, but it is also a carnivore, which is an animal that eats other animals. Animals that eat only plants are known as herbivores. Animals such as humans eat both plants and meat. They are called omnivores.

Vertebrate Animals

Birds	Fish	Amphibians	Mammals	Reptiles

• Have feathers • Breathe air • Warm-blooded • Lay eggs with hard shells	• Have scales • Breathe in water with gills • Cold-blooded • Lay eggs with soft shells	• Spend lives partly in water and partly on land • Cold-blooded • Lay eggs with soft shells	• Have hair/fur • Breathe air • Feed young with mother's milk • Usually bear live young	• Dry skin and scales • Breathe air • Cold-blooded • Lay eggs with tough shells

What are the basic needs for survival?

All living things need food, water, shelter, and space in order to survive. Plants change sunlight, water, and carbon dioxide into food during a process called **photosynthesis**. Plants use the food to grow flowers, fruit, leaves, and roots. The fruit contains seeds, which will become the next generation of the plant. Animals eat plants to nourish their bodies so they can grow, repair injuries, and produce young.

Not all plants require the same amount of water to survive. Most desert cacti need little water. They can store water to use during long dry spells. Water lilies grow with their roots submerged in water. Animals get some water from their food. Deserts have less animal and plant life than forests or coral reefs.

The photosynthesis of green plants provides the basic energy source for almost all organisms.

Not all animals and plants can survive in extreme climates. Trees do not grow near Earth's polar regions because it is too cold and windy for most of the year. Low-growing lichens grow well on the northern tundra. Animals need shelter from harsh weather and a place to hibernate during winter. A snug den or nest is required to raise young and provide protection against enemies. People need shelter, too. Houses keep people safe and comfortable.

Space is important for both animals and plants. In crowded conditions, plant roots cannot develop properly. Animals may not have enough food to go around.

BYTE-SIZED FACT The moon snail lays eggs in a curved, gray, "collar" shape on West Coast beaches. The eggs are enclosed in jelly that provides food and shelter until they hatch.

How Do Scientists Study Wildlife?

How is it possible to study something you cannot get close to or even see?

Wildlife watching has gone high tech. Scientists use technology to collect data while animals perform their normal activities in the wild. The tools they use include radio collars, satellite tags, and leg bands with tiny electrical transmitters. Some of these things even work underwater, such as video cameras attached to sea lions, which allow scientists to observe their eating habits. Machines that allow scientists to clearly hear sounds underwater, called hydrophones, are used to listen to the sounds made by orcas. Some methods used by scientists are not high tech at all. For example, a dab of brightly colored paint on a polar bear allows scientists to identify the bear from an aircraft.

Animals and birds may be captured so scientists can attach tracking devices. Large animals may be shot with darts containing drugs to stun them or make them sleepy. Birds are trapped in fine nets. These animals are handled carefully and released as soon as possible to avoid harming them.

Using these devices, scientists learn about life cycles, **population** numbers, how far animals travel, what they eat, how long they live, and how they die.

This data may be collected by satellite and analyzed by a computer before they are studied by researchers. The results increase scientists' knowledge and understanding of wildlife so they can better preserve species and their habitats.

BYTE-SIZED FACT Miniature satellite tags are so lightweight they can be attached to a small bird or butterfly to track its movements.

How high can you count?

No one knows exactly how many organisms live on Earth. Scientists estimate that between 10 million and 100 million species may exist, but they have only identified a small fraction, about 1.4 million. Even fewer species have been studied. Scientists think they have identified most birds, flowering plants, and large mammals. Smaller creatures, such as invertebrates, exist in staggering numbers. It is possible that there are more than 30 million invertebrate species. New species of invertebrates are discovered daily, especially in tropical rain forests, where the greatest variety of animals and plants live.

The variety of living species on Earth is known as biological diversity, or biodiversity. How did so many species come to exist? They resulted from the abundance of different habitats, or **niches**, on Earth. Over long periods of time, organisms particularly suited to a certain niche survived to pass

Organisms and their environment constantly interact. Even small changes in an ecosystem can determine if a plant or animal will be successful in its environment.

along their traits to future generations. Organisms less suited to the niche died out. This gradual process, called natural selection, eventually results in a group of very similar organisms (species).

These organisms share traits that allow them to live and reproduce successfully within their niche. It may take millions of years for a new species to emerge, but natural selection is happening all the time.

BYTE-SIZED FACT More than 20,000 different types of orchids live in the world's rain-forest environments.

The Mysterious Lemming

The mouse-like lemming lives in northern climates. Its population reaches peak numbers about every four years. The next year, however, lemmings are usually scarce. Why do their numbers decrease so suddenly? Where do all of these lemmings go? Biologists are not sure.

It is possible for some animals to reproduce too quickly, causing populations to exceed the habitat's ability to feed and shelter them. For a long while, people believed that when lemmings became overpopulated, masses of them ran into the sea and drowned. This theory may have come about because people in Scandinavia observed that lemmings living in mountainous regions would travel downhill through valleys to bodies of water. In the Canadian Arctic, most lemmings live on the tundra far from the sea coast. However, in years when the populations are high, some lemmings have been seen unusually close to the sea.

Many mammals, birds of prey, and snakes feed upon the lemming.

This has contributed to the idea that lemmings run toward water when they become too crowded. But it is just as likely that, during times of scarcity, lemmings simply wander far from their normal habitats in search of new feeding grounds.

So far, all of the ideas about why lemming populations rise and fall are just theories. No one has been able to prove that lemmings are driven to commit suicide because of overpopulation. Today, most scientists believe that changes in the numbers of lemmings are from other causes, such as changes in the numbers of their predators, changes in their food supply, or diseases.

BYTE-SIZED FACT

In a mass extinction 65 million years ago, Earth lost about two-thirds of its species, including dinosaurs. Some scientists believe that as many as three-quarters of Earth's species may be extinct or endangered by the year 2200.

What happens if you can't change your ways?

Not all species remain on Earth forever. Many have vanished since life began on this planet. Some scientists estimate that species are disappearing at a rate of about 70 per day. Others believe the number is closer to 135 per day.

An animal population may be at risk if it is very dependent on one thing for survival. For example, the monarch butterfly needs the milkweed plant. It must lay its eggs on the milkweed because it is the only plant species its **larvae** can eat. When the larvae are fully grown, they spin their cocoons on the milkweed. In places where milkweed no longer grows, the monarch butterfly can no longer live.

A seabird called the marbled murrelet nests in old-growth forests, mainly near the west coast of Canada. The birds fly out to sea at night to feed. An old-growth forest is a mature, complex, and diverse forest community. It can be made up of birds, herbs, insects, mammals, shrubs, and trees. Scientists are trying to preserve the remaining areas where these trees grow in order to save the murrelet.

The monarch butterfly is poisonous to other animals. It obtains this poison from the milkweed plant when it is a caterpillar.

BYTE-SIZED FACT

Millions of monarch butterflies migrate to Mexico each fall from southern Canada and the United States. So many perch on tree trunks that their weight sometimes breaks branches.

Here is your challenge:

Human beings can live in almost any part of the world. They can live in most climates and environments. How is this possible? List some of the ways humans have learned to adapt and survive successfully.

Ornithologist

Birding, or bird-watching, is one of the fastest growing pastimes.

For some, it is more than a hobby; it can become a career. Roger Tory Peterson (1908–1996) turned his own boyhood delight in watching and drawing birds into a lifetime career as an ornithologist (someone who studies birds). Peterson studied art at college and later taught art and science. When he began writing about birds, his books included detailed paintings. His first book, the well-known *A Field Guide to the Birds*, was published in 1934. The book taught millions of birders to identify different species by spotting key features, such as colors, beak shapes, or wing marks.

The Roger Tory Peterson Institute of Natural History is located in Jamestown, New York. The institute offers exhibits, programs, and events that encourage visitors to learn about the natural world.

Ornithologists around the world admire Roger Tory Peterson. His work made people more aware of wildlife and the need for conservation of bird species and their habitats.

BYTE-SIZED FACT

Every year at Christmas, bird counts are held across North America to collect valuable data on bird populations. The practice of recording the number of bird species viewed replaced bird hunts. Held until 1900, bird hunts were activities in which any birds spotted were killed.

Do people and nature always get along?

Some human beings use Earth's living resources for profit. Some species have become endangered from overuse or **exploitation**. African elephants are hunted for their ivory tusks, which are used to make items such as jewelry. Alligator skin is prized for purses and shoes. In the past, human beings have exploited species for food— sometimes to the point of extinction.

At one time, passenger pigeons lived in enormous flocks across North America. It is estimated that there were two billion passenger pigeons in one flock. In flight, a flock this size would have been 1 mile (1.6 km) wide and 300 miles (482 km) long. Over time people discovered that the young pigeons were good to eat. Beginning in the 1850s, thousands of these birds were killed.

Why do you think people continue to use real snakeskin when imitation snakeskin is widely available and much less expensive?

They nested in colonies of up to 90 nests in a single tree. Hunters killed whole colonies in a short time, taking all of the young birds. Because female pigeons laid only one egg each year, it was not long before no passenger pigeons were left to continue the life cycle. By the 1880s, the population that once numbered about five billion had declined to a few hundred. The last passenger pigeon known to exist on Earth was a bird named Martha at the Cincinnati Zoo. Martha died in 1914, marking the end of a species.

Here is your challenge:

Find another example of a species of animal or plant that is endangered or extinct because of the actions of humans. To learn more about endangered species try visiting www.wwf.org (World Wildlife Federation), www.endangered.fws.gov (The Endangered Species Program, U.S. Fish and Wildlife Service), or www.cites.org (Convention on International Trade in Endangered Species of Wild Fauna and Flora).

Conservation Officer

Are you concerned about wildlife and the environment? Do you like spending time outdoors? A conservation officer's job is to help protect and preserve natural resources such as wildlife.

A key role of a conservation officer is to enforce laws that people who hunt and fish for sport must obey. If a complaint is made against someone who hunts out of season or without a license, the conservation officer investigates, gathers evidence, and may arrest the violators and send them to court. The officer takes special safety training classes to learn how to properly handle weapons such as guns.

A conservation officer learns a great deal about wildlife and may assist biologists in the protection of animals. If a bear wanders into a city, the conservation officer is called upon to tranquilize and remove it. Sometimes, the officer might also be asked to speak to groups interested in the outdoors.

Often, conservation officers must take care of animals that have been badly injured by careless or illegal hunters. With the help of a conservation officer, many animals recover from their injuries.

Does Earth really need all these species?

With so much biodiversity on Earth, some people might wonder what difference it makes if some species become extinct. Over millions of years, many life forms have developed and become extinct. Scientists do not know anything about these life forms or whether they were an important part of the ecosystems in which they lived.

People should care about biodiversity because human beings depend on animals and plants for food. Scientists also use the **genetic material** found in certain wild plants to develop new crops that are easier to grow or that produce more food. With each extinct species, important diversity is gone forever.

Many plants provide people with medicines, too. About one-quarter of all prescription drugs have ingredients that come from the natural world.

In addition to nature's importance to human health, it also improves people's lives in other ways. Humans value nature for its beauty and the enjoyment it brings. Humans create works of art using animals, birds, and flowers as subjects. People take part in **ecotourism** to see rare plant species or unusual wildlife. Human lives would be less rich without the diversity that nature offers.

Without plants, the planet would quickly run out of oxygen for people and animals to breathe.

Only **1** percent of the world's plants have been tested for use in medications.

Here is your challenge:

Take a survey of your family or friends. How many recreational activities can you list that depend on the natural ecosystem? Do not forget to include the equipment you might need for these activities and the material used to make this equipment.

Tourism and Ecotourism

Tourism to places of natural beauty is a popular pastime and an important source of income for the people living in the areas that attract visitors.

However, large numbers of tourists cause changes to the environments they visit. Resorts built for tourists replace parts of the natural landscape, contribute to pollution, and disrupt animal and plant life.

Over time, many people recognized the problems of tourism, and they began to develop a new way of traveling called ecotourism. Ecotourism is defined by The International Ecotourism Society (TIES) as "responsible travel to natural areas that conserves the

On some safaris, local guides will drive visitors to see animals up close in their natural environments. Should this be considered ecotourism?

environment and sustains the well-being of local people." Often, the money brought to such areas by ecotourists helps support the endangered ecosystems.

Ecotourists can take a boat tour to see whales during their migration along the West Coast of North America. They can also take a safari in an African wildlife preserve, where animals such as elephants and lions are protected from hunters.

The whooping crane can be taken

as one example of how ecotourism has helped both species and local people. This bird spends its winters at a refuge on the coast of Texas. The presence of the cranes draws many tourists and helps keep local store owners in business.

The rain forests of Costa Rica in Central America are another popular ecotourism destination. Visitors spend millions of dollars each year enjoying the fascinating Costa Rican ecosystems, but there are special rules about where tourists can go and how they should behave to help preserve the rain forests.

BYTE-SIZED FACT

By 1941, the migratory population of whooping cranes was a mere 16 birds owing to hunting, human disturbance, and collecting. In 2003, the whooping crane's total population was about 300. In addition to the wild flock, four small captive flocks now live in Maryland, Wisconsin, Texas, and Alberta, Canada.

Spaces

"There's no place like home."

The "eco" in ecosystem comes from a Greek word meaning "house." In modern English, "eco" means "the place where things live—their environment or habitat." An ecosystem is the space living things call home, and it is one of the basic needs of all life forms. A natural environment suitable for life forms includes air, land, and water. It might contain grasslands, mountain slopes, desert sands, or tropical rain forests that are thick with vegetation. Earth's many environments fit together like a large jigsaw puzzle. Some pieces may be cities, which are artificially created urban habitats for human beings. Other pieces may be droplets of water, each one providing a home for a certain species of **microorganism**. Environments continually change, sometimes for natural reasons and sometimes because of human activities.

What is meant by a "suitable environment"?

An environment is suitable for life to exist only if the right conditions are present. Earth's environment includes air, soil, and water. Typical weather conditions such as temperature, wind, rainfall, and sunlight determine the environments in which different species are able to survive. For example, a butterfly cannot survive an Arctic winter. A mountain goat prefers steep slopes to avoid predators. Fish cannot exist out of water. A change to the environment will affect the number or kinds of animals and plants living there.

Many species need to live in more than one environment. They migrate as the seasons bring lower temperatures that destroy their food supply. They return when conditions are favorable again. Swallows spend the summer in North America and the winter in South America. They must leave their northern habitat when plants stop growing and insects die. They return in the spring as soon as the first flying insects hatch.

BYTE-SIZED FACT

An unexpected environmental change, such as a cold snap in late spring, can mean death for birds that migrate earlier in the year than other birds. Freezing temperatures kill insects, and without this source of food, birds can starve in just a few days.

Sharp-rimmed hooves with a rubbery sole keep mountain goats from slipping on steep or slick surfaces.

Where on Earth do organisms live?

Scientists have categorized the Earth's environments into different ecosystems, also called **biomes**. Some are land-based, but there are water biomes, too. Land-based biomes are named for their main plant species, which provide habitats for many living things. The type of plants or vegetation in each area depends on the climate, soil, and elevation. Humans are a factor too, because people can change these environments and create artificial ones.

The Major Land-Based Biomes

Name	Location	Characteristics
Tropical rain forest	near the equator	dense vegetation, high biodiversity, warm and wet
Temperate forest	areas with cold winters	**deciduous** trees, rich soil, limited number of animal species
Boreal forest or taiga	areas with short summers located in the far North	mainly **coniferous** and old-growth trees, furry animals, many birds
Grassland	bordering forest areas	natural grasses, herbivores, alternately dry and wet
Desert	areas typically near the tropics or North and South Poles	deeply rooted plants, few animals or birds, low rainfall, very hot or very cold
Tundra	in mountains above tree line, around Arctic polar region	low, shallow-rooted plants, cold permafrost, few animals

The Major Water-Based Biomes

Name	Location	Characteristics
Ocean	71 percent of Earth	plants near the surface, varied animal life, salty water
Inland waters	lakes, ponds, rivers, wetlands	still or flowing water, varied biodiversity, fresh water

A Butterfly Conservatory

There is little chance of seeing many of the world's estimated 200,000 species of moths and 18,500 species of butterflies in the wild. Thanks to technology, humans can walk among some of them at any time of the year—indoors.

Scientists use technology to duplicate the habitat of tropical rain-forest butterflies in a climate-controlled space called a conservatory. Computerized heaters keep the glass-covered dome at 80°F (27°C), and humidifiers, or machines that add humidity (moisture) to the air, keep the atmosphere wet like a rain forest. Visitors wander pathways that follow trickling streams. Flowering plants are grown for their nectar and pollen, which butterflies eat. Butterflies lay their eggs on the leaves.

The Butterfly House at the Melbourne Zoo has about 800 individual butterflies belonging to 12 different species. Like other butterfly houses, the goal is to educate people, study butterfly habits, and breed endangered species.

Fruit and sugar solutions at feeding stations provide extra food. Pesticides are not used. Instead, helpful insects patrol the conservatory and prey on any harmful pests that appear.

Entomologists, or people who study insects, have learned how to raise many butterfly species. Through windows to special hatching areas, people can watch the adult insects emerge from cocoons after undergoing **metamorphosis**. A butterfly life cycle takes about two weeks to complete. Depending on the size of the dome, there may be several thousand butterflies on display at one time. Some are brought from butterfly farms in Central and South American countries or the South Pacific. No wild butterflies are captured for the exhibit.

BYTE-SIZED FACT
Many butterflies that are red, orange, yellow, and black are poisonous if eaten. Some harmless species share these colors to fool predators.

How big are ecosystems?

As long as it provides the basic needs for its inhabitants, an ecosystem can be any size.

A single drop of water is an ecosystem for microscopic organisms. Nutrients in the water are used for food. Organisms will die if the water is too hot or too cold. For example, humans boil water from some sources because most organisms cannot survive in extremely hot water. This kills harmful bacteria, making the water safe to drink.

A coral reef is an ecosystem found in warm, shallow ocean water. It consists of vast colonies of tiny animals called **polyps**, which have limestone shells. The reef is a habitat for hundreds of fascinating species, including fish, sea anemones, sponges, and sea horses.

The Great Barrier Reef is a large coral reef that stretches for 1,250 miles (2,000 km) along Australia's northeast coast.

Earth is the largest known ecosystem, containing countless species and habitats. All of the basic needs for life are found within the atmosphere of our planet.

BYTE-SIZED FACT

The boreal forest (also called taiga forest) is Earth's largest land-based ecosystem. The mixture of coniferous and deciduous trees forms a ring around the top of the globe between grasslands and tundra, broken only by areas of ocean.

Urban Planner

Would you like to plan a city?

Creating an artificial environment such as a city takes careful planning. This is the job of an urban planner. An urban planner studies the design of a populated area to understand how the land is being used for buildings, transportation systems such as roads or subways, and green spaces.

Urban planners must consider a city's future needs. They must determine when new shopping malls or schools need to be built. They also need to consider how people will travel from new neighborhoods in the suburbs to the downtown business district. They might work to completely change or renew older parts of a city. Parks for recreation are important in an urban setting, too. Some natural ecosystems, such as wetlands or woodlands, must be protected from pollution. Sometimes wildlife corridors are located within cities. Corridors are areas of natural habitat that wildlife use to travel from one place to the next.

Most urban planners work with the local government to develop long-term and short-term plans for land use. They must consider social, economic, and environmental issues while developing plans for community growth.

To help make decisions, urban planners often collect data and organize it with a computer. They analyze the data and use this information to write reports or create maps. The urban planner shares this information with land developers and government officials, and often the public, too. Together they can decide what a city will look like in the future.

What happens when a mountain blows up?

Natural changes to the environment happen often. It may take a long time before humans can see the effects. Gradual change in the temperature and amount of rain may mean fewer plants can grow. Less vegetation means less food and shelter for animals. They must adapt, move to other areas, or die out.

Other kinds of changes, such as a natural disaster, can suddenly disrupt an environment. If vegetation is destroyed by heavy rains, soil can erode. Sometimes landslides occur. When such changes occur, animals may no longer have the food and shelter they need to survive. A dramatic example of a suddenly changing environment was the May 1980 volcanic eruption of Mount St. Helens in Washington state. The blast threw thick clouds of ash miles into the air and devastated 230 square miles (595 sq km) of forest. The closest plant life was scorched or buried. Some birds were able to escape. Small mammals

In 1982, the U.S. Congress created the 110,000-acre (45,000 hectare) National Volcanic Monument to include the area around Mount St. Helens so that it can develop naturally and provide opportunities for study and education.

were killed immediately or died later because their food, water, and shelter were gone. Some coniferous trees survived the blast because they were protected by late spring snow. They spread their seeds quickly. Roots left from other burned plants soon created new growth. As plant life gradually returned, animals moved back to the region. Bird species, such as woodpeckers, returned to use nest cavities in the dead trees. Clearly, the environment went through an enormous change, but the area was able to stabilize over time, and animal and plant life adapted to the new conditions.

BYTE-SIZED FACT

A South Pacific volcano, Krakatoa, erupted in 1883. It was the largest eruption in recorded history. The eruption produced so much ash that it caused unusually red sunsets and lower temperatures worldwide for three years.

Decaying Log

A living tree provides a habitat for many animals and plants. Once it dies, a tree is still very useful. The environment changes, but plenty of living things depend on a dead tree for survival.

Decomposers in a dead tree speed up the process of decay. Meanwhile, small animals and birds still find suitable homes inside holes in the trunk. Beetles live under the bark. Fungi grow in cracks that appear as the wood dries out. Once the tree falls onto the damp ground, earthworms and various insects feed on it. Birds may no longer be able to live in it, but small mammals such as rodents can. A chipmunk might leave a seed in its nest inside the tree trunk. If the seed sprouts, the young plant takes root in the rotting wood that has become as soft as soil. The old tree returns to the earth. The new one starts the cycle of life all over again.

Decaying hollow logs provide places for animals to hide their young or to take shelter from predators.

Here is your challenge:

Start your own ecosystem by making a worm composting box or building a compost bin in your garden. Ask for help at a garden center, or find a library book with information about composting. Compost is a mixture of decaying organic matter, such as decomposing leaves, manure, and certain kitchen scraps. It is used for fertilizing soil. Composting reduces the amount of household garbage families produce, helping to save space in landfills. How long does the material take to decompose into soil? Hold your hand over the pile. Why is it warm?

How does human activity affect the environment?

Human activity is responsible for many harmful changes to the environment. Humans turn forests into cities and grassland into airports, destroying the natural habitats of many other species. Humans also fill in wetlands to create more land for crops or buildings. Habitat destruction is a leading cause of the loss of biodiversity.

Cutting down large areas of forest causes soil erosion, destroys animal habitats, threatens the survival of species, reduces biodiversity, and changes the climate.

Use of **fossil fuels** like coal, oil, and gas has led to air pollution, causing a worldwide problem known as global warming. Scientists believe Earth's temperature is increasing. If global warming continues at the current rate, major environmental changes could occur. For example, the polar ice caps could melt, causing coastal areas to flood. This is a problem for humans, animals, and plants.

Chemical pollution has increased as the human population has grown. More and more, humans use toxic substances, such as fertilizers, that stay in soil and water for many years. Animals and plants cannot avoid these chemicals in the environment. If the chemicals seep into drinking water, they can harm humans, too.

BYTE-SIZED FACT

A disease called hantavirus increased in parts of the United States in the early 1990s. It was caused when changes in land use and climate reduced the number of coyotes and other animals that eat rodents. The population of deer mice exploded. Deer mice can be carriers of the hantavirus disease, which can infect humans. Larger numbers of deer mice resulted in more humans getting the virus than ever before because the mice moved into homes and buildings. This increased the chances of contact between mice and humans.

Piping Plover

Can wildlife and people share the same environment?

One tiny shorebird competes for beach space with summer tourists. The piping plover nests in April along the East Coast of North America. Few areas provide the right combination of food and sandy beaches for these birds to nest. Using broken shells and pebbles, the female lays four eggs in its shallow nest in May. Both parents share the job of sitting on the eggs for 28 days. The chicks leave the nest in July, four weeks after they hatch. Since July is peak season for vacationers who flock to the popular beaches, these birds are at high risk. The parents and chicks have little defense against people, pets, and vehicles.

The piping plover received endangered species status under the Endangered Species Act in 1985. The nesting areas are listed as critical habitat so they are protected through policies that prevent them from being disturbed.

If the chicks do not survive, that year's population is lost. The piping plover is now a threatened species. Scientists believe only 6,000 birds inhabited Canada and the United States in 2001.

Biologists are coming to the rescue. On some beaches, the plovers' nesting area is fenced off until the chicks can fly and move to safer spaces. Piping plover numbers have increased 17 percent in 5 years in the United States. These efforts are improving the situation, but tourists should still watch where they step on the beach.

Relationships

"Everything in its place."

Earth's ecosystems run like finely tuned machines, with each part depending on the rest to function as expected. A single change can affect the whole system. If the balance is thrown off in an ecosystem, it can have major effects on all of the individual parts. Scientists investigate the cycles in nature to understand what keeps things in balance. Science provides the tools to restore order when something goes wrong.

How does a balanced ecosystem work?

All organisms in an ecosystem are interdependent. They are connected to each other by their needs. Each living thing uses, or is used by, another living thing. This is nature's way of keeping ecosystems in balance.

Trees use nutrients in the soil to grow. When they die and fall, they decay, and the nutrients are returned to the soil. Many animals use trees. Some spend their entire lives in them. Birds shelter in holes in tree trunks or build nests among branches. They might feed on insects living in the same tree, helping to prevent damage to its leaves or bark. Some insects pollinate a tree's flowers so that fruit or seeds will be produced.

All plants and animals play a vital role in a balanced ecosystem. For example, if too many trees are cut down, birds and squirrels lose their homes and food sources. If they die, the animals that depend on the squirrels and birds may also starve.

Mammals such as squirrels sometimes nest in trees and climb their limbs to travel from place to place. While gathering pine cones from coniferous trees, squirrels scatter the seeds so that new trees will grow.

The more biodiversity an ecosystem has, the more links there are between its inhabitants. Often these links are related to food through food chains and food webs.

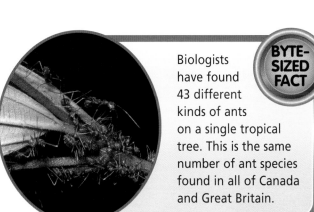

BYTE-SIZED FACT

Biologists have found 43 different kinds of ants on a single tropical tree. This is the same number of ant species found in all of Canada and Great Britain.

Exploring Underwater Ecosystems

Humans cannot live underwater. However, deep-sea and SCUBA diving technology allows scientists to study ecosystems in an environment very different from their own.

Humans use breathing equipment called SCUBA (Self-Contained Underwater Breathing Apparatus) to breathe and dive underwater. A device called a regulator controls the airflow to match the pressure in a diver's lungs with the water pressure. A wet suit made from waterproof fabric keeps a diver warm. A mask keeps water out of the diver's eyes. Divers wear rubber fins on their feet to make swimming easier. To collect information, a diver may use an underwater camera or sound recorder. Other electronic equipment allows the diver to communicate with the boat crew at the surface of the water.

Scientists dive to study underwater animals, plants, and land formations. They explore marine sanctuaries to identify species, count populations, and learn about effects of pollution on biodiversity in an underwater ecosystem.

The ocean is considered Earth's final frontier. As better technology is developed, scientists are able to dive deeper and make new discoveries.

Breathing equipment for diving was first tested in the late 1800s. However, it was not until 1943 that Jacques-Yves Cousteau and Emile Gagnan developed a successful compressed air device, the aqualung, which is the basis for SCUBA equipment used today.

BYTE-SIZED FACT

What is a food chain?

All living things need food for energy. This need links them together like a chain. Plants are the first link on a food chain. They are called **producers** because they are able to convert the Sun's energy into a form that animals can use. Plants are eaten by animals, known as **primary consumers**. These animals are eaten by other animals called **secondary consumers**. When producers and

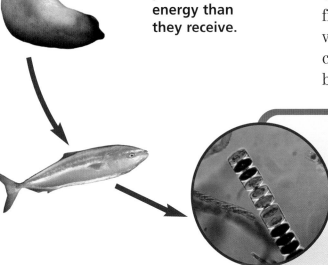

Organisms in each level of a food chain pass on less energy than they receive.

consumers die, their tissues are broken down by the final link in the food chain, decomposers.

A food chain in the Arctic might begin with microscopic ocean plants called phytoplankton. These tiny organisms take the nutrients they need from the sea. Phytoplankton are eaten by sea-dwelling creatures such as copepods, tiny relatives of lobsters and crabs. Shrimps called krill eat the copepods. Krill is a favorite food for seals, which are eaten by polar bears. The polar bear is at the top of the chain, meaning that it has no natural enemies. When the polar bear dies, scavengers and bacteria will consume its body. It will be changed into nutrients, many of which will be washed back into the sea where they will be used by photoplankton. The food chain has come full circle.

Most animals are part of more than one food chain. For example, seals eat fish as well as krill. Krill is also eaten by whales, linking them to yet another food chain. When chains connect, they become a food web.

Seaweed, together with phytoplankton, form the basis of the food chain in the sea. Many small animals feed on seaweed. These small animals are eaten by larger animals. Seaweed's height can range from 1.5 inches (4 cm) to 164 feet (50 m). It is an ingredient in everyday products such as pet food and toothpaste.

BYTE-SIZED FACT

What is a population cycle?

A cycle is the orderly way events occur in nature. In a cycle, the end of the process leads back to the starting point, much like a circle. In Earth's water cycle, for example, water is lifted from lakes and oceans by **evaporation**. It falls back to Earth as rain or snow, eventually draining into bodies of water. Then it evaporates again to continue the cycle.

Some animals are so closely linked in a food chain that their population increases and decreases in a regular cycle. Scientists have learned that the lynx and its main prey, the snowshoe hare, follow this kind of **population cycle**. Over a period of nine to ten years, hares in a community produce enormous numbers of offspring. This makes hunting easy for the lynx. Soon, the lynx eats so many hares that the number of hares drops. With less of their favorite food available, the number of lynx drops, too. When the population of this predator declines, populations of hare begin to increase again. This increase is followed closely by an increase in the lynx population. These cycles continue, and the ecosystem stays in a balanced state.

Habitat destruction, hunting, or the introduction of a new species can disrupt a population cycle. It can take species years to recover from an imbalance.

Atlantic Cod Fishery

Human ways of life often have a negative impact on natural ecosystems. Humans may depend too heavily on a natural resource, with drastic results to the environment.

Fishing for Atlantic cod was a common way of life for generations of residents on the eastern coast of the United States. Whole families fished or worked in fish-processing plants. Cod was the main source of income in many small communities.

In the mid-1950s, fishers began to notice that they were catching fewer fish. The cause of this was not completely understood. A combination of factors probably led to the crash of the cod populations.

One theory is that large factory ships from many countries had been catching millions of fish from the Grand Banks off the coast of Newfoundland, one of the world's richest fishing grounds. Technology helped the ships locate the largest schools of cod. Perhaps changes in the environment were also part of the problem. Around the same time, waters in the Grand Banks were unusually warm, causing cod's main food source—a fish sensitive to temperature changes called capelin—to become scarce.

Large ships called trawlers hauled nets across the bottom of the Grand Banks, disturbing the habitat and parts of the food chains that fish depended on.

In 1992, so few cod were being caught that governments stopped people from fishing them. This meant the end of a major source of income for many people and whole communities. Until the cod ecosystem is restored, the East Coast cod fishery no longer exists.

Despite laws against cod fishing in both Canada and the United States, cod populations have failed to return to their previous level. There have been demands to reopen the fisheries after slight increases in numbers, but doing so could further threaten the cod ecosystem.

What is a keystone species?

Scientists believe animals such as the California sea otter may be keystone species in an ecosystem. If the keystone is removed, the delicately balanced system falls apart.

While all species in a habitat depend on each other for survival, some species play a more important role in maintaining the quality of the habitat. If these keystone species are removed or disappear from a habitat, the connection between that species and others in the habitat begins to change.

The sea otter is a West Coast mammal that lives on floating kelp beds. Its main food is spiny sea urchins from the ocean floor. Prized for its fur, the sea otter was hunted in the 1700s until it was believed to be extinct. Since otters were no longer eating sea urchins, the sea urchin population soon increased, and the urchins ate kelp until it too was gone.

Kelp beds provide a habitat for many marine creatures. These creatures are food for fish. Kelp also softens the force of waves, keeping the shore from eroding during storms. Some surviving sea otters were found living farther north along the coast. They were brought back to places from which they had disappeared, and were protected by the government. The sea urchin had a predator once again. As sea urchin numbers fell, the kelp began to grow. The natural balance in the ecosystem was restored.

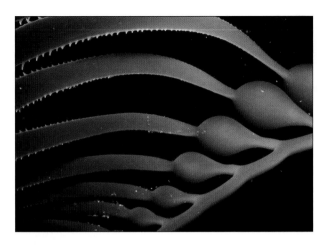

People use kelp in many products such as ice cream, cosmetics, herbal remedies, and plant food.

The sea otter can eat 25 to 35 percent of its body weight in one day. The sea otter eats a wide variety of foods, including spiny sea urchins.

BYTE-SIZED FACT The sea otter population was once estimated to be at 300,000. When it was finally protected in 1911, only 1,000 to 2,000 remained. Today, it has rebounded to about 150,000 animals.

Rain Forest

What is a rain forest without rain?

For decades, the Amazon rain forest has been getting smaller. Humans are destroying it bit by bit. Trees are cut and burned to make space for cattle ranching or farming. This is how the people living in this area make money. Unfortunately, the removal of large numbers of trees threatens to destroy this important ecosystem.

When a rain forest is left undisturbed, all the parts of the ecosystem work to keep itself in balance. For example, the many trees reflect 3 percent to 10 percent of the sun's radiation. Their shade cools the air and land beneath them.

As part of the water cycle, water moves from plants to

the air. The air is cooled, moistened, and rain falls.

Rain lands on forest canopies, which slow its trip to the ground. The soil has time to soak up rainfall gradually, providing more water for trees.

When the trees are removed, the air and land become warmer and drier. Less rain falls, but it reaches the ground faster. Soil is washed away with no tree roots to hold it. Once

If rain forests continue to be destroyed at current rates, they will be gone in less than 100 years, along with most of the world's plant and animal species.

nutrients are gone, the remaining soil cannot support plant life. Without plants, animals have no food or shelter. The ecosystem has changed so drastically that it may never be replaced.

Loss of rain forests affects the whole world. Burning of the trees adds to air pollution. There are fewer trees to use carbon dioxide and replace it with the oxygen organisms need to survive.

BYTE-SIZED FACT

Temperate forest species may have a home range of hundreds of miles. Rain-forest species may live in an ecosystem the size of a football field. This means that destroying even a small patch of rain forest can potentially wipe out an entire species, not just a few individuals. This is why loss of the rain forests has a much greater effect on biodiversity than similar damage to other types of habitats.

Can endangered species be saved?

Animals can sometimes be returned to a former environment that was disrupted by humans. The peregrine falcon was seriously threatened until the 1960s by a poisonous chemical called DDT. This colorless chemical pesticide was sprayed on crops to kill harmful insects. Falcons, which are at the top of their food chain, ate small birds that ate insects sprayed with the pesticide. The DDT caused falcons to lay eggs with shells so thin that they broke before the young could hatch. This threatened the population of peregrine falcons. After DDT was banned in North America, biologists learned how to raise the endangered birds in artificial nest boxes. Placed on top of city skyscrapers, the boxes imitate a falcon's natural cliff habitat. The peregrine falcon is on its way back from near extinction, although it may still encounter the deadly pesticide in its South American wintering grounds, where DDT is still used.

The peregrine falcon was listed as endangered in 1970 under the Endangered Species Conservation Act. Thanks to massive recovery programs throughout the country, the bird was taken off the list in 1999. The peregrine falcon's amazing recovery makes it one of the most dramatic successes under the Act.

BYTE-SIZED FACT

The golden toad was once commonly found in cloud forests in central Costa Rica, but none have been seen since 1989. The region they lived in was once covered in clouds and mist, but this climate has become warmer and less moist. Scientists believe this change may have caused the outbreak of diseases, such as skin fungi, that were not previously a problem for the frogs.

POINTS OF VIEW

Are National Parks for Wildlife or People?

National parks are some of the only places where larger animals can still live under somewhat natural conditions. They are also some of the best places for people to see these animals in the wild. Many people want more roads built in parks so they can reach remote areas to view wildlife and participate in recreational activities such as camping. Other people support mining and logging in parks to take advantage of their natural resources.

Should national parks be kept as natural as possible for

the wildlife they protect, or should they be made easier for people to use? Should people take natural resources from parks?

"We have here the second largest wilderness park in the world. There are just so many things to see and do. I think people from all over would come if they had a means of traveling through the park." **Mayor of a community near a major national park**

"The desires of some visitors threaten to destroy the substance of the parks themselves or are in direct conflict with the desire of other visitors for high-quality experience." **Legislative representative of a conservation association**

"This mine would be an environmental catastrophe . . . a barrier to wildlife movement in . . . an important natural corridor." **Naturalist**

"I believe access should be limited to the public and shut off from industry. Preserving wetlands, grassland, [and mountain] ecosystems is the only way of ensuring that endangered species still have a place to live." **President of a naturalists' club**

How do you think national parks should be used?

Biologist

Who collects information about living things and how they work together? What tools do they use?

If you are interested in learning about Earth's ecosystems, you might want to work in the large field of science called biology. There are many different jobs for biologists. They may work outdoors in a nature center or zoo, carry out experiments in a lab, or work with museums to help create realistic displays.

Biologists usually concentrate on one species or environment. For example, marine biologists investigate life in the ocean. Ornithologists study

birds. Entomologists explore the insect world, and botanists deal with plants. Experiments lead to many of the answers biologists seek, as well as more questions. Biologists make small changes to the environment, a plant, or an animal so they can observe how it is affected by these changes. A microscope is one of their most useful tools.

Biologists can work with governments, private corporations, research firms, universities, and conservation groups.

Computers help to sort out the facts and compare results. A biologist's work is important to all living things. The discoveries they make can help natural ecosystems, as well as improve the lives of humans.

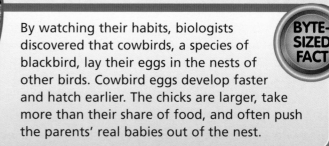

By watching their habits, biologists discovered that cowbirds, a species of blackbird, lay their eggs in the nests of other birds. Cowbird eggs develop faster and hatch earlier. The chicks are larger, take more than their share of food, and often push the parents' real babies out of the nest.

BYTE-SIZED FACT

POINTS OF VIEW

Should Wildlife Be Captured, Tagged, or Radio-Collared for Study?

Scientists observe animals to learn about their behaviors and life cycles. They find clues that may alert them to problems with the health of the environment. To collect accurate data, scientists may capture, tag, and then release animals and birds. Large animals may be drugged to calm them, then measured and radio-collared. Birds are trapped in nets, or their nests are closely watched so the number of eggs they produce can be counted.

Some people feel these methods are necessary to learn how animals live so we can better protect them and preserve their environments. Others believe these treatments cause too much stress to the animals, sometimes even causing their death.

"As caretaker for these animals, [we strive] to do the best possible job of managing them properly so there will always be populations in existence." **Biologist**

"You shouldn't be doing things you can't justify. Sometimes in the field you have to make that kind of determination and say, 'No, this isn't right.'" **Wildlife technician**

"We follow strict guidelines for handling the bears, and minimize trauma by getting all the basic information at once." **Biologist**

"There have been so many studies, they must know everything there is to know about those caribou. There's just too much of it going on." **Spokesperson for a group of native peoples**

How do you feel about this method of studying wild animals?

Your home is a type of ecosystem. Your family is a community of living things depending on each other. Some members work (producers) for money to buy food for all (consumers) to eat. Your house may be an artificial environment, but it is still your habitat. It may be easy to forget that you are part of nature. If you take a look around your home, you will find clues about how you and your family fit into a larger ecosystem.

How do you fit into an ecosystem?

1. Look in the refrigerator. Do you see food items that come from nature? Can you think of food chains or food webs that include you?
2. Turn on the tap of the sink faucet. What part do you play in the water cycle? Do you know where the water you drink comes from? Where does the water go after your family uses it?
3. Look in your room. Did any of your furniture come from nature? What about your clothes? Which items are made from artificial materials?
4. What makes your house a comfortable environment? Do you depend on plants or animals for shelter, warmth, or protection?

Survey Results

People may be able to make many of the things they need, but humans are still closely connected with nature. All of our food comes from plants or animals. We use and reuse the same water as all other living organisms in the world—there is only one supply for every living thing. Our furniture may come from trees (wood) and our clothes from plants (cotton) and animals (wool, leather). The heat and electricity we use are produced using gas or other fuels found in nature.

The process of removing wool from sheep is called shearing. The wool is cleaned and woven into strands or balls that can be dyed to make items such as clothing and blankets.

Fast Facts

1. Temperatures in tropical rain forests can reach more than 100°F (38°C). The air may be 20°F (7°C) cooler under the canopy of the trees.

2. The large marine iguanas that inhabit the isolated Galapagos Islands are the world's only lizards that spend time in ocean water. They feed underwater on seaweed and lichens.

3. A rain-forest inhabitant, the emerald tree boa, spends its whole life in the trees where it waits for its prey.

4. The Serengeti Plain in Tanzania is home to nearly all of Africa's best-known species of large mammals, such as lions and wildebeests.

5. Biodiversity increases on all continents near the equator, but it decreases near the poles.

6. The largest animal group on Earth is insects. It is estimated to include more than 751,000 different species.

7. Amphibians, vertebrate animals that live part of their lives in fresh water and part of their lives on land, are found on every continent except Antarctica.

8. The bald eagle is the only eagle that is unique to North America. Habitat destruction and illegal hunting are two reasons it is considered an endangered species in most of the United States.

9. The world's greatest diversity of turtle species is found in India.

10. The soft-bodied hermit crab lives in the discarded shells of other animals.

11. The California condor is an endangered species. These condors once existed in great numbers, but their population declined as the human population increased. Poisoned food sources, power lines, and hunters have contributed to this decline.

12. Mangroves are trees that grow in swampy areas. Forests of mangroves are keystone habitats. With their shallow root systems often extending above water, mangroves provide safe areas for many land and water species to live.

13. A bird called the Hawaiian honeycreeper has adapted to the diversity of food in its habitat and has evolved over time into 50 different species.

14. Beetles are the largest insect group. About 300,000 species have been identified.

15. Cockroaches have been around for more than 350 million years. They can live in almost any habitat and eat almost anything.

16. Fleas are parasites. They live on warm-blooded organisms and have tough bodies that are hard to crush.

17. Spiders play an important role in keeping a balance in the insect population. They use poison and sticky webs as tools to catch their meals.

18. The West Indian manatee population has decreased to such a degree that it is considered an endangered species. The decline was originally caused by overhunting of the animal for leather, meat, and oil. Today, many manatee deaths result from collisions with boats and barges.

19. New animal and plant species are continually discovered in the world. In 1991, the pygmy beaked whale was discovered off the coast of Peru. In 1990, a new species of monkey, the black-faced lion tamarin, was found in Brazil.

20. On the island of Borneo, 1 square acre (0.4 hectares) of rain forest commonly contains more tree species than all of North America.

Young Scientists@Work

Test your knowledge of ecosystems with these questions and activities. You can probably answer the questions using only this book, your own experiences, and your common sense.

FACT:
Interdependence means everything is connected to everything else.

TEST:
See how acid rain affects plants in an ecosystem.

MATERIALS:
• Two spray bottles
• One measuring cup
• Distilled water
• 1 cup (240 mL) vinegar
• Adhesive labels
• Two small, healthy plants of the same size and species

1. Fill one spray bottle with distilled water and label it "water."
2. Pour 1 cup (240 mL) each of distilled water and vinegar into the other spray bottle. Label it "acid rain."
3. Label one plant "water" and the other "acid rain." Place them in a warm, sunny window.
4. Every day for three weeks, spray the plant leaves and keep the soil moist. Use only the water spray bottle on the water plant, and only the acid-rain spray bottle on the acid rain plant.

OBSERVATIONS:
What differences do you see between the two plants?
How might acid rain affect a different ecosystem, such as a field of corn?

FACT:

Clean water is one of the basic needs of all living things. The water cycle cleans Earth's supply of water.

TEST:

See how nature cleans water.

MATERIALS:

- Water mixed with soil
- One large bowl or plastic dish pan
- One glass or plastic cup
- Plastic wrap
- A small pebble

1. Place a few inches of muddy water in the pan.
2. Set the cup in the middle of the pan.
3. Cover the pan with plastic wrap. The edges must seal tightly but must not be stretched too tight.
4. Place the pebble on the wrap over the cup. The wrap should dip slightly.
5. Set the pan in direct sunlight for a few hours.

OBSERVATIONS:

Where does the clean water in the cup come from? Try this test again, leaving the pan in a dark place. Do you get the same result? Why?

Research on Your Own

Do you want to know more about ecosystems and biodiversity? Check your library or the Internet for these excellent resources. Here are some great books and websites to get you started.

Great Books

Farndon, John. *Wildlife Atlas: A Complete Guide to Animals and Their Habitats.* New York: Reader's Digest, 2002.

Gallant, Roy A. *Wonders of Biodiversity.* New York: Benchmark, 2002.

Godkin, Celia. *Sea Otter Inlet.* Toronto: Fitzhenry & Whiteside, 2001.

Wallace, Holly. *Food Chains and Webs.* Chicago: Heinemann, 2001.

Great Websites

Biomes of the World
http://mbgnet.mobot.org

Kids in the Hall of Biodiversity
http://www.amnh.org/nationalcenter/kids/kids_
    bio/index.html

World Wildlife Fund Kids Stuff
http://www.worldwildlife.org/fun/kids.cfm

Glossary

biodiversity: the variety of different species of plants and animals in an environment

biomes: major ecological communities, such as grassland or rain forest

classification: process of grouping organisms by their similarities

coniferous: type of tree that produces cones

deciduous: type of tree with leaves that fall off each year

decomposers: organisms that break down the cells of dead plants and animals into simpler substances

ecotourism: the practice of touring natural habitats in a way that will not affect them negatively

evaporation: the changing of a liquid into a vapor

exploitation: making unfair use of something mainly for one's own advantage

fossil fuels: fuels that come from the ancient remains of plants and animals

genetic material: chemicals in a cell that determine the traits passed from parents to offspring

interdependent: the state of depending on another being or thing, and being depended upon

larvae: the immature, wingless, feeding stage of an insect that undergoes complete change

metamorphosis: a major change in form from one stage to the next in the life cycle of an organism

microorganism: any living thing that is so small it can only be seen using a microscope

natural resources: materials supplied by nature

niche: unique place occupied by a species in its habitat

organisms: living things

photosynthesis: in green plants, the process of converting sunlight, carbon dioxide, and water into sugar in the presence of chlorophyll

polyps: invertebrate animals that live in large colonies and create coral reefs

population: a group of organisms inhabiting a particular location

population cycle: regular changes in the size of a population

primary consumers: herbivores that feed on producers

producers: organisms, such as plants, that are able to produce their own food from nonliving substances

secondary consumers: carnivores that feed on herbivores

species: organisms of the same or similar kind that can breed together to produce offspring that can also breed

Index